School RULES!

tips, tricks, shortcuts, and secrets to make you a super student

by Emma MacLaren Henke
illustrated by Stacy Peterson

★ American Girl®

Published by American Girl Publishing

All rights reserved. No part of this book may be used or reproduced in any manner whatsoever without written permission except in the case of brief quotations embodied in critical articles and reviews.

16 17 18 19 20 21 22 LEO 10 9 8 7 6 5 4 3 2 1

Editorial Development: Mary Richards Beaumont
Art Direction & Design: Wendy Walsh
Production: Jeannette Bailey, Virginia Gunderson, Cynthia Stiles
Illustrations: Stacy Peterson
Photography: cover, Grafner/iStock/Thinkstock
Special Thanks: Tanya Zempel

Library of Congress Cataloging-in-Publication Data
Henke, Emma MacLaren, author.
School rules! : tips, tricks, shortcuts, and secrets to make you a super student / by Emma MacLaren Henke ; illustrated by Stacy Peterson.
pages   cm
ISBN 978-1-60958-743-7 (pbk.) — ISBN 978-1-60958-762-8 (ebook)
1. Schools—Juvenile literature. 2. Study skills—Juvenile literature. 3. Students—Conduct of life—Juvenile literature. I. Peterson, Stacy, illustrator. II. Title.
LB1556.H46 2016   371—dc23   2015021249

americangirl.com/service

Dear Reader,

From the time you're five years old—or even before—until you're pretty much grown up, you will be a student. It's your job to learn. And whether you're one of a thousand kids in your school or a home-schooler studying with siblings, the same rules apply. You've got to read and take notes. You'll prepare for tests, write reports, and figure out tricky problems. You'll love some subjects and find others a challenge.

Knowing how to approach school can make your life a lot easier. And this book can help you create habits for staying organized and focused so that you'll get more out of school. Use a separate notebook to take the quizzes and complete the writing projects—that way, you can use the book over and over as the school year goes on.

What's the number one rule for school success? Strive to be the best student you can be. You don't need to be perfect. But if you give school your best effort, you'll learn more—and have more fun doing it, too!

Your friends at American Girl

contents

LET'S GET ORGANIZED!

Order and preparation can clear your path to great grades.

A Place For Everything

Sort through these questions to see how your organizational skills stack up.

1. You keep your bedroom neat, your closet clean, and your clothes crisply folded in your dresser drawers.

Sounds like me.   **That's not me.**

2. Your friends want to take a cartooning class Tuesdays and Thursdays after school. You sign up on the spot, without checking your calendar. Your schedule won't suffer, right?

Sounds like me.   **That's not me.**

That's not me.

3. Every school night, you pack your lunch before you get ready for bed. You never run out of your favorite snacks because you always add them to the family grocery list well before they're gone.

Sounds like me.   **That's not me.**

4. At least once a week, you can't find something that you need right away. It's never in the place it should be!

Sounds like me.   **That's not me.**

5. If your mom peeked in your backpack, she might find a broken pencil, a granola bar wrapper, and a bunch of folded-up papers you were supposed to give to her weeks ago.

Sounds like me.   **That's not me.**

6. You never miss a project due date because you write them all in your assignment notebook.

Sounds like me.   **That's not me.**

answers

Did you choose **blue** the most? You're one orderly girl! You already know that staying organized makes life easier. Your skills will help you stay on top of your game at school, even when you have to tackle tricky topics or when your schedule is packed with assignments and activities.

Did you select a few **orange** and a few **blue**? Like most of us, you're organized at times and disorganized at others. When it comes to school, keeping order frees up your mind so you can focus on learning. If you're organized, you're not distracted by the perfect pencil you can't find or the due date you know is coming up sometime soon (you think).

Did you pick mostly **orange** answers? Your organizational skills could use a tune-up. Keep this in mind: School isn't just about learning subjects like science or reading. School teaches life skills, too. And a couple of the most important skills you learn through school are how to be responsible for your own things and how to manage your time. Read on to find out how to get organized!

super study space

What tools do you use for homework and studying?
Gather your supplies and keep them close by when you're working.

Keep track of how long
you spend on any task.

Keep a generous stash
of your favorite pencils
and pens.

Use sticky notes in books, on your
calendar, and on your assignments to
mark important details or give yourself
reminders. Also, notecards are
great to have on
hand to make
quick flash cards.

Eraser

Try using a white or pink eraser
to remove pencil marks cleanly
and completely.

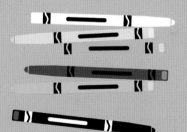

Always note due dates, tests, and performances! Use a calendar and your assignment notebook to make sure you're getting everything done.

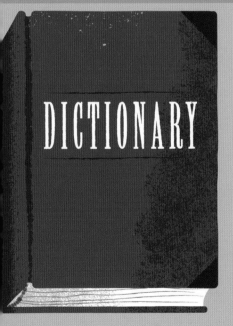

Twistable crayons and colored pencils never need to be sharpened.

It's OK to use a calculator to double-check your homework as long as you solve arithmetic problems on your own first!

Read a word you don't know? Look it up!

STUDY STEADY

Studying in the same place at the same time creates a habit that will seem natural in no time. If you have your own desk, keep your school tools organized in the drawers or right on top. If you usually study at the kitchen table or another shared space in your home, make a school supplies kit in a sturdy box and get it out every time you sit down to do homework or study.

Wherever you work, choose a place that's quiet and free from distractions. That's right: no buzzing phone on your desk so you can check your texts. No TV blaring in the background. No noisy little brother begging you to play a game.

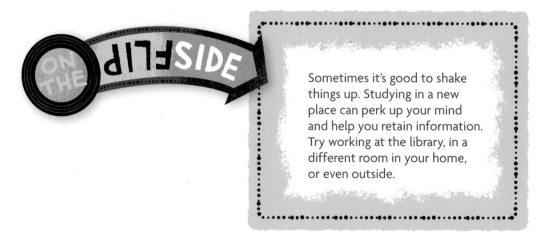

ON THE FLIP SIDE

Sometimes it's good to shake things up. Studying in a new place can perk up your mind and help you retain information. Try working at the library, in a different room in your home, or even outside.

IS TIME ON YOUR SIDE?

Get right to these questions to
see if you tend to *procrastinate*—
that is, to put things off until the last minute.

1. Your report on Mexico is due tomorrow.
   This evening you still need to . . .

   a. proofread what you've written one last time.
   b. take a look at one last website, and write the final page of your report.
   c. research and write the report.

2. It's only one week till Halloween! Your costume . . .

   a. has been hanging in your closet for a month.
   b. still needs a few finishing touches.
   c. will come together sometime soon— why worry about it now? You've still got a week.

3. If your spelling test is Friday, you study the words . . .

   a. Monday and again on Thursday.
   b. Wednesday or Thursday after the rest of your homework is done.
   c. Friday morning, on the school bus. Might as well make use of the ride time!

4. You take piano lessons on Tuesdays after school. You practice piano . . .

   a. for a few minutes every day.
   b. after your lesson Tuesday, while the music is fresh in your mind, and a couple more times during the week when you get the chance.
   c. Monday night and Tuesday morning. You feel ready for your lesson— sort of, at least—if you practice right beforehand.

5. If you have a week to complete a challenging math assignment, you . . .

   a. do as much as you can over the week-end, when you don't have much other homework and you can concentrate and figure out the tough problems.
   b. do a problem or two every day and finish up the remaining work the night before the assignment is due.
   c. get to work after dinner the day before the assignment is due. You like to think you do your best work under pressure.

answers

Did you choose . . .

Mostly a's? You understand the perils of procrastination. Good for you! If you put off a job until the last minute, you might not have time to give your best effort. You understand just how good it feels to get your work done ahead of time.

Mostly b's? You don't intend to put things off, but sometimes that's what happens. Remember, it's as important to organize your time as it is to organize your materials. Planning your time for each task and sticking to your schedule will help keep you from procrastinating.

Mostly c's? You probably already know that you are a procrastinator. You put off tasks you need to do until the last minute. You may tell yourself that you do good work when you feel the pressure of a deadline. But what happens when you run out of time to get a job done? Practice planning your time. Break big jobs down into small tasks that you can complete, one at a time. Make a schedule for doing each small task.

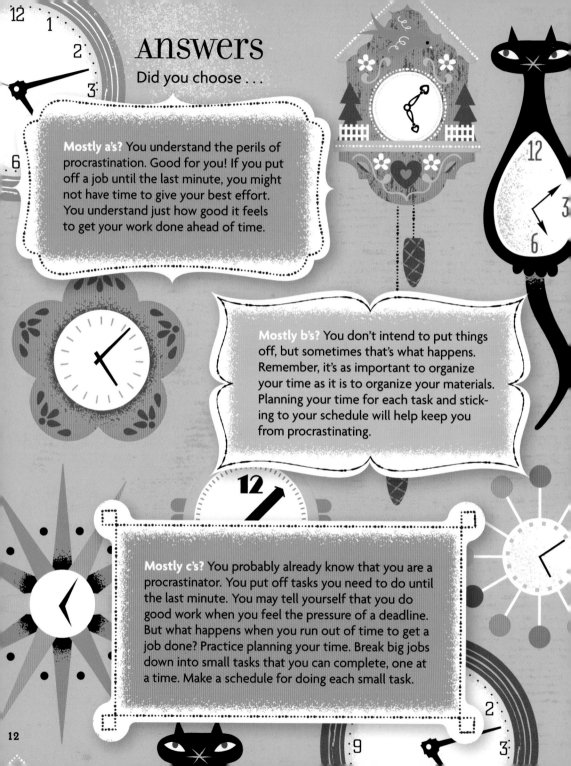

TOP TIPS FOR procrastinators

1. Plan to get done early, not right on time.

2. Use a kitchen timer to motivate yourself for short bursts of effort. Set the timer for 5 or 10 minutes (or whatever feels right to you) and don't let yourself be distracted from the task at hand until the timer beeps. Just keep on working.

3. Use a planner or calendar. Make sure to note due dates and test times, but also plan out what you need to do each day to get the job done.

4. Ask your family to check in about your progress on big projects.

5. Get started! Just digging in can be the hardest part of any task, especially one you don't enjoy.

calenDar GIRL

Feeling puzzled about how to squeeze everything you need to do into your busy schedule? Use a calendar, planner, or assignment notebook to see how all the pieces of your school life fit together.

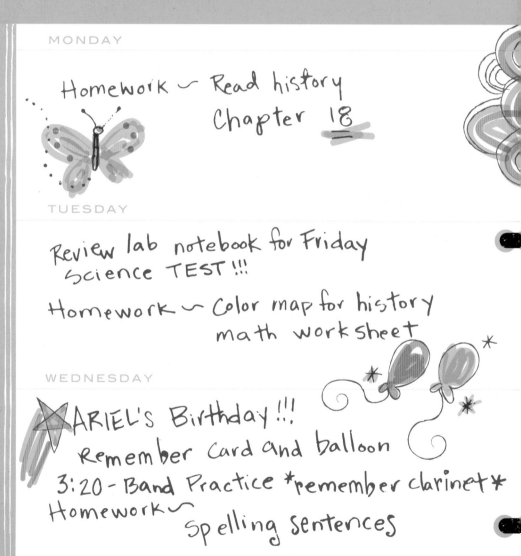

MONDAY

Homework ⌣ Read history
Chapter 18

TUESDAY

Review lab notebook for Friday
Science TEST !!!

Homework ⌣ Color map for history
math worksheet

WEDNESDAY

ARIEL's Birthday !!!
Remember card and balloon
3:20 - Band Practice *remember clarinet*
Homework ⌣
Spelling sentences

Review science flash cards
Homework ∿ math worksheet

SCIENCE TEST!!!
3:20 - Band Practice * clarinet *

NOTES

- Note all **test days** and project **due dates.** Write down what you need to do each day to prepare for upcoming tests or projects.

- Note **practices,** performances, and games.

- Write down each homework assignment **clearly** and completely—that's always worth the time it takes. Check off each assignment when it's completed.

- Use colored pens or highlighters to make your pages more **fun** to look at!

PERFECT PACKING

Create a checklist to make sure you bring everything you need home from school and back again. Don't forget books, forms, and permission slips!

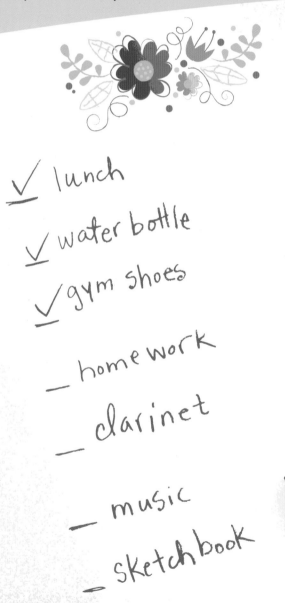

✓ lunch

✓ water bottle

✓ gym shoes

— homework

— clarinet

— music

— sketchbook

READY, SET, STUDY!

Learn how you learn, and become a homework pro.

WHaT'S your STUDY STYLe?

Pinpoint your learning style to make the most of your study sessions. Choose as many answers as you like.

1. You like to study for spelling tests by . . .

    a. writing out your words.
    b. spelling your words out loud.
    c. looking at your words in your spelling book.

2. Your favorite topic in math class is . . .

    a. math facts, because you love to practice with a partner.
    b. geometry, because the shapes help you see math ideas clearly.
    c. story problems, because the words show how to use math in real life.

3. To learn how to bake your favorite cookies, you'd . . .

    a. study the recipe in the cookbook, then try it yourself.
    b. ask your dad to make them with you and show you what to do.
    c. watch a video recipe online.

4. You'd prefer to find out how water freezes by . . .

    a. studying your science textbook.
    b. listening to your science teacher explain the process.
    c. making ice cubes and observing them as they freeze and melt.

5. Your favorite teachers tend to . . .

    a. give exciting lectures.
    b. assign interesting reading.
    c. create cool projects.

9. For the science fair, you'd choose an experiment that requires . . .

a. reading lots of background material.
b. creating diagrams and posters.
c. working with a group.

10. To memorize a poem, you'd . . .

a. write the poem over and over until you knew it by heart
b. say the poem out loud to yourself and ask others to read it to you.
c. read the poem again and again, covering up lines to see if you remember them.

6. You're studying presidents in history class. You'd like to find out more by . . .

a. reading an essay.
b. reviewing a graph.
c. taking part in a class discussion.

7. Your teacher recommends a book to the class. You'd love to . . .

a. read the book right away.
b. listen as the teacher reads the book to the class.
c. put on a skit that brings a scene from the book to life.

8. The activity you'd choose in Spanish class is . . .

a. practicing conversation with a group of friends.
b. watching Spanish language cartoons.
c. writing stories using new Spanish vocabulary words.

answers

Take a look at the choices you made. Each color shows a way you like to learn. Understanding your learning style helps you find techniques for homework and studying that work for you.

Red: You're a **visual** learner. You learn by taking in information with your eyes. Reading textbooks and looking at charts and diagrams help you make sense of new ideas.

Green: You're an **auditory** learner. You learn by hearing new information. When your teacher tells stories or explains new ideas out loud, they really stick with you. You like to study what you're learning by saying it out loud or making up a story about it.

Purple: You're a **hands-on** learner. You learn by doing. You like science experiments, physical activities, playing music—anything where you take an active part in learning new skills. If information comes in the form of words, you learn it best when you write it out yourself.

Pink: You learn through **people.** Sharing ideas with a cooperative group and hearing others' thoughts help you process information.

Orange: You learn through **words.** You enjoy reading, writing, and speaking. You use language to organize your ideas. Thinking about ideas in terms of sentences may help you to remember information.

Blue: You learn through **pictures.** Creating pictures in your mind helps you remember new information. You're good at understanding ideas presented in diagrams, illustrations, and movies.

ON THE FLIP SIDE

You're probably most comfortable learning in one or two different ways. But that doesn't mean those are the only ways (or even the best ways!) for you to learn. Practicing a study method that makes you a bit uncomfortable can produce results. Forcing your brain to process information in a new way can help you remember the information. So don't get stuck in a study rut. For example, use math flash cards one day, write problems down the next day, and say them out loud to yourself the next.

Homework Hero

Does homework drag you down? Follow these tips to soar through your studies.

NO TIME LIKE THE PRESENT

It's good to take a break after school: Have a snack, do something physical, or just relax. But don't let too much time pass before you start your homework. You never really know how long your homework will take, and you want to make sure you can get it done. Set a time frame for when you plan to start your homework each day. If you do after-school activities, include those in your plan.

PREVIEW, REVIEW

Read through your assignment completely before you begin. Scan all the math problems you'll be working on to see if you understand them. Read the history questions you'll have to answer before you read the section assigned in your history text. Skim the chapter of your science book before digging in for a thorough read. These techniques help you know what to look for when you're reading and studying.

TRICK WITH A TREAT

Use mini rewards to motivate yourself to complete homework tasks. For example, if you finish a page of math problems, take a two-minute break to check your phone or grab a snack or snuggle your pet. Then, get back to work.

SUBJECT SWITCH

When you start to feel "burned out," change the subject you're working on. If you feel really frustrated with your writing homework, for instance, stop writing and practice math facts instead. Come back to the challenging subject when you've completed the rest of your work.

CLASS ACT

Homework doesn't always go as planned. If you can't get your work done or if you're having trouble understanding what to do, make sure to talk to your teacher. Teachers know that on some nights, homework goes undone because of family responsibilities or events outside your control. And sometimes you just don't get it. Homework is supposed to help you learn. Teachers want to know if you get stuck. Talk to them!

CHECK YOUR WORK

When you're done, you've just begun! When you finish an assignment, check to make sure you followed directions, fully completed the assignment, and labeled your paper with your name and the date. Check your answers, too.

ASK A FRIEND

Sometimes you need help to make homework happen. Make a list of friends in your class you can talk to when you forget an assignment, when you want to double-check directions, or when you're just plain stumped.

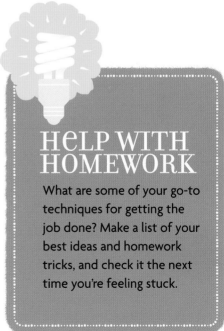

HELP WITH HOMEWORK

What are some of your go-to techniques for getting the job done? Make a list of your best ideas and homework tricks, and check it the next time you're feeling stuck.

Neat Freak!

When it comes to homework, neatness counts. But how much? Take this quiz to find out if you spend too much time keeping up appearances.

1. Your book report is due tomorrow. Tonight, you spend the evening . . .

   a. carefully copying your favorite illustration from the book to give your report the perfect look.
   b. flipping through the book you read to add important details to your report.
   c. playing video games, after you spend a few minutes scribbling down some sentences about the last book you read.

2. Drat! You discover your science homework crumpled up at the bottom of your backpack. Before you turn it in, you . . .

   a. copy your work over to a crisp new sheet of paper, even though that means you hand in your assignment a little late.
   b. smooth it out as best you can and double-check your work for errors.
   c. just dig it out of your backpack.

3. Your math homework looks like . . .

   a. it was printed by a computer, even though it's just your best handwriting.
   b. you understand it's important to show all your work and check your answers.
   c. a swirl of numbers, scribbles, and eraser marks.

4. You're completing the final draft of a social studies essay. Your teacher tells you to make sure to polish your writing, so you . . .

   a. use your best, most careful penmanship as you copy your second draft.
   b. think about the main idea of your essay and change your writing so that everything you say supports your main idea.
   c. cut out the three sentences your teacher marked in your second draft. That should take care of the problems she found!

5. In art class, you usually . . .

   a. find you're the last person to complete your project. You spend lots of time making every detail look just right.
   b. complete your projects on time and feel satisfied with your artwork.
   c. race to complete your projects so you have time to doodle.

Sometimes it's OK to be a bit sloppy! When you're sketching, freewriting, or brainstorming, focus on getting your ideas down, no matter how your paper looks. Other school tasks call for you to put most of your effort into neatness and presentation: Just think about cursive practice. Mostly, though, solid content is the key to successful schoolwork. Remember, your work is supposed to show how well you understand what you're learning, no matter what subject you're studying.

answers

Mostly a's

Neat Freak

You place a high value on the visual presentation of your schoolwork—and that's great. But don't get carried away with worry about how your homework looks. Don't compromise correct, complete, thoughtful answers just to show off your pretty penmanship or neat drawing.

Mostly b's

Neatness Counts

Your schoolwork usually strikes a good balance between presentation and content. You're good at showing what you know clearly and thoroughly.

Mostly c's

Not the Neatest

You get your work done, but neatness is not your top priority. Keep in mind that first impressions are important. If your teacher sees your work as sloppy and careless, he or she may think the content of your ideas is sloppy and careless, too.

MIND Games

Use mnemonics to make memory your superpower.

A *mnemonic device* (nih-MAH-nik) is a tool or trick that can help you remember something. There are many kinds of mnemonics.

Some mnemonics use a silly saying or sentence to list the words you need to remember. The first letters of the words in the saying match the first letters of the terms you need to remember, like an acrostic. For example, you can use the phrase "Never eat soggy waffles" to remind yourself of the points on the compass: north, east, south, and west. This kind of mnemonic helps with spelling, too. To spell the word *mnemonic*, for instance, you could remember the silly sentence, "Many nights each mouse opens new ice cream."

Mnemonics sometimes use the power of rhyme to make facts stick in your brain: Think of "I before E except after C" or "In 1492, Columbus sailed the ocean blue."

Other mnemonics use *acronyms,* or words made up of the beginning letters of other words. Perhaps you've heard the name Roy G. Biv. This acronym helps you remember the colors of the rainbow in order—red, orange, yellow, green, blue, indigo, violet—by making a name out of the first letter of each color. Or, think of the word *HOMES* to remember the names of the five Great Lakes: Huron, Ontario, Michigan, Erie, and Superior.

Create custom mnemonics for whatever you need to study. Give it a try! Come up with your own mnemonics to remember . . .

. . . how to **spell** the word *weird*.

. . . the **names** of the last five presidents.

. . . items you **need to bring** home from school—such as your gym shoes, lunch box, notebook, and art project.

Many
nights
each
mouse
opens
new
ice
cream

MUSICAL MIND

Can you remember the words to your favorite song? Of course! Music can give your memory a burst of strength. Whether you have to memorize a speech, a list of dates, spelling words, math facts, or anything else, music can help. Try singing the facts you need to learn to a familiar melody such as "Happy Birthday" or "Twinkle, Twinkle, Little Star."

abc

LETTER PERFECT

The next time you're sure you know the name of a person or place, but you can't think of it, try this trick: In your mind, go through the letters of the alphabet, slowly, in order. Think about whether the word you're searching for begins with each letter. Consider, "Does it start with A? Is the first letter a B? Is it C? D?" and so on. Chances are, you'll recall the information you need when you land on the right letter.

SEEING IS BELIEVING

Making pictures helps you understand new ideas.

You learn through images every day. Think how many maps, illustrations, diagrams, and drawings appear in your textbooks or on the walls of your classroom. Creating pictures yourself is a great way to check if you understand what you're studying. Drawing diagrams and sketches helps you organize information and gives you a new tool to remember what you learn.

See how pictures explain these ideas:

MULTIPLICATION
4 x 2 = 8

THE SOLAR SYSTEM

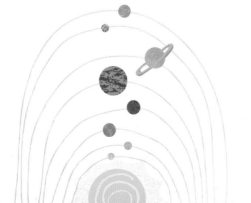

VOCABULARY
brittle: dry and easily breakable

hobgoblin: a trouble or worry

orchard: an area of land devoted to the cultivation of fruit trees

Make a list of ideas for using drawings, diagrams, and other images in your own schoolwork.

YOU'VE GOT CLASS

Learn how to make the most of time with your teachers.

TALKING POINTS

Whether class discussions make you clam up or sing like a bird, these do's and don'ts will help you talk your way to success.

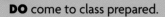

DO come to class prepared.

DO volunteer information to add to the discussion.

If you're shy, **DO** come to class with a question you wrote down in advance. Try to ask your question early in the discussion.

DON'T think only about what you want to say next, tuning out what others are saying.

Tell a joke?

I thought I meant...

DON'T dominate the discussion.

DON'T steer the discussion away from the teacher's topic.

DO follow class rules for discussion: If you're supposed to raise your hand before you speak, do so.

DON'T say anything personal about another student or put down another student's ideas.

Take Note!

Pack more meaning into your notes for better learning now and later.

Why do teachers want you to take notes in class? You may think you take notes so you can study them when you prepare for a quiz or a test. And that is true.

But did you know that **just the act of taking notes** helps you learn, too?

When you write information down, the information goes into your brain in a new way. You **hear** what your teacher says. You **see** what your teacher writes on the board or shows on a map or diagram. When you **write** down the main ideas you see and hear, your mind takes in those ideas in a third way. The more ways information goes into your brain, the stronger your learning!

NO-NONSENSE NOTES

- **Always** date and label your notes.

- **Keep notes** for each subject in separate notebooks.

- **Write down** main ideas. Don't try to capture every word. You don't need to write in complete sentences.

- **Use outline format.** Under each topic or main idea, write the points that pertain to it or support it.

- **If you hear** your teacher saying something more than once, it's probably important. Write it down.

- **Listen for key words** such as "reasons," "examples," "important," or "first, second, third." Also listen for dates and names. Write down the reasons or examples your teacher gives. You'll need to study these ideas.

- **Copy information** your teacher writes on the board.

- **Write down** the three D's: definitions, dates, and diagrams.

- **Write down** any questions you have. Make sure to ask your questions at the end of class or at another appropriate time.

- **Use highlighters** to color-code important information.

Teacher's Pet or Teacher's Pest?

Take the time to find out whether you're a thoughtful classmate.

1. When a teacher asks a question and I know the answer, sometimes I shout it out without raising my hand.

   Could be me.   I'd never do that!

2. My pencil case might be filled with notes, gum, and a bunch of unsharpened stubs. That's OK, though, because my teacher always has extra pencils on hand.

   Could be me.   I'd never do that!

3. Sometimes I wait until the very last minute to ask to go to the rest room. Then I *have* to go, no matter what's happening in class.

   Could be me.   I'd never do that!

4. If I forget my homework, I might tell the teacher a fib like "My mom accidentally threw it in the trash" instead of owning up to my mistake.

   Could be me.   I'd never do that!

5. When I get back a test with a good grade, I might celebrate and shout out, "Yeah! Rocked it!"

   Could be me.   I'd never do that!

6. If I've got something really important to say to my best friend, I'll whisper it to her in class, even when the teacher is talking.

   Could be me.   I'd never do that!

7. If I make a mess eating a snack or working on an art project, I don't worry about it. The school has custodians, right?

   Could be me.   I'd never do that!

8. If my teacher points out something I'm doing wrong in an assignment, I might sigh, roll my eyes, and sulk around for the rest of the day.

   Could be me.   I'd never do that!

9. I cram all my papers and textbooks into my desk. If the lid closes, who cares what it looks like inside?

Could be me.   I'd never do that!

10. I might laugh out loud if the teacher or another student makes a silly mistake.

Could be me.   I'd never do that!

SUPPLIES   FOLDERS

Eraser

I'd never do that.

answers

Take a look at the choices you circled. If you picked "Could be me" for any of the situations, think about how your classroom behavior affects others. Remember, your classroom is a space you share with other students and your teacher. You must work together to be considerate of one anothers' needs. Your teacher's time is limited—when you waste it, you're wasting it for all your classmates, not just yourself. You share school materials such as books and desks with other students. Do your best to treat them with respect and keep them clean. Most important, think about how your actions might make others feel. With luck, they'll do the same for you!

ROTTEN APPLES

Want the inside scoop on how not to behave?
We asked teachers to share their classroom pet peeves.

Not listening.

When students blame every forgotten object on **Mom and Dad.** "Where's your homework?" I ask. "My mom left it on the kitchen table," says my student.

Skipping **directions** on tests or assignments.

Interrupting!

When students **wait until the last minute** to ask to use the bathroom and then have to go during a test or while I'm giving important instructions.

Nose picking!

When students raise their hands and then, when I ask what their question is, say "**I forgot.**"

When students forget to put **their names** on their papers!

When one student shouts out the answer to a question that I specifically asked **a different student.**

When **students tattle** on other students just to get them into trouble.

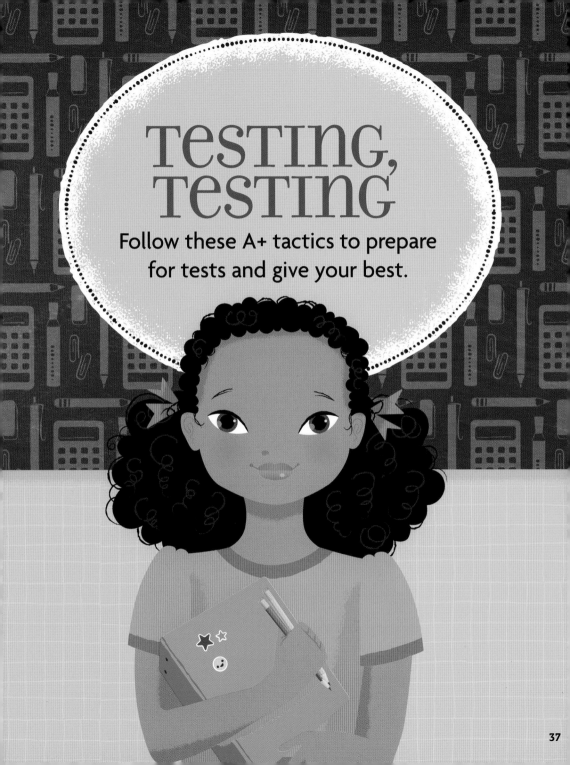

TESTING, TESTING

Follow these A+ tactics to prepare for tests and give your best.

Proper prep

Getting ready for a big test? Use these tips to earn top marks.

TIMING IS EVERYTHING

Plan to space your study sessions throughout the week before your test. For instance, if you know you have a test on Friday, look over your notes the Sunday before, quiz yourself on the material on Tuesday, and do a final review on Thursday. Studying over a period of time will help you learn more than cramming for exams at the last minute. Your brain needs rest between study sessions to absorb information and form new ideas about what you're reviewing.

SEE THE FUTURE

Take time to think about what's going to be on your test. Here are a few great places to look for clues:

- Textbook **review questions** at the end of each chapter

- **Bold print,** underlines, or exclamation points on handouts from your teacher

- Important points in your class notes, especially **names and dates**

Make a list of the questions and big ideas you find, and use your list to study.

Do you know what kind of test you're taking? Will it be multiple choice? Will it be timed? It doesn't hurt to ask. You might prepare differently for an essay test than you would for a true/false quiz. If your teacher will tell you what the test is like, make up your own practice questions in that format and try to answer them.

MIND MAP

Make a list of the main items you need to know. For example, if your test is on government, list the topics you studied. Then, write one item (a name, a term, an idea) from your list at the center of a blank piece of paper and circle it. Write everything you know about that item around the circled word. Draw lines to connect these details to the center word. Connect the details to each other where it makes sense to do so.

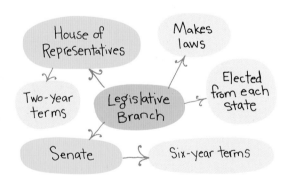

Be the Teacher

If you can teach it, you probably know it. So try teaching test material to a sibling or parent. See if you can answer their questions at the end of your tutoring session.

STUDY IN A FLASH!

Flash cards count as double-dip studying. You review material when you use the cards, but you also review when you *make* the cards!

Flash Forward

Make your own flash cards to test yourself on the material you need to know. Flash cards work well for learning definitions and capitals, matching people and accomplishments, or matching events and dates.

Or, take a blank sheet of notebook paper and draw a line down the center. List terms you need to know on one half and their definitions on the other, dates you need to learn on one half and what happened on the other, and so on. Fold the paper in half so you see only one column. Quiz yourself, and flip the paper to check your answers.

annual	happening once a year
biennial	happening every other year
centennial	relating to one hundred years; one-hundred-year anniversary
perennial	constantly recurring; happening again and again
bicentennial	two-hundred-year anniversary

great Games

These cool contests take your study group from drills to thrills.

QUIZ QUEST

Play this study game with a group of friends—it's like having your own game show!

To set up: On note cards, write questions, problems, or prompts you need to know for your test. List the answers to your questions on a separate sheet of paper. Number questions and answers so that it's easy to match them later. Write a point value from 1 to 5 on the back of each question card, giving easy questions lower values and harder questions higher values. Make sure you assign equal numbers of each point value.

To play: Lay out your cards in rows with the point values facing up. The person who creates the questions acts as answer judge. One player starts by choosing a card, turning it over, and reading the question aloud. The first player to answer correctly keeps the card and chooses the next card. When the cards are gone, players add up the points on the cards they've collected. The player with the highest score wins.

① Name the five planets closest to the sun.

Fact or Fiction?

Learn with a familiar game: Two Truths and a Lie. Play with your study group.

To set up: Each player writes a list of facts you need to know for your test as well as a few incorrect statements—the *fiction*—about the material you are studying.

To play: Players take turns reading two facts and one incorrect statement to the group. The other group members write down which piece of information they think is fiction. Then the speaker reveals the answer. Players earn one point for each fictional statement they identify. The player with the most points after each player has had three turns as speaker is the winner.

COOTIE CATCHER QUIZ

Use a folded fortune-teller as a study tool! Fold paper into a cootie catcher. On the outside layer of your folded paper, write four different numbers. On the next layer, write eight questions or prompts (one on each small triangle) for a topic you need to study. On the innermost layer, write the matching answers. Quiz yourself or your study partners.

HOW TO FOLD a COOTIE CATCHER

Cut off the top part of a piece of printer paper so that what's left is a square.

1. Fold and unfold the paper in half diagonally in both directions to make an X. Fold each corner point into the center.

2. Flip so that flaps are facedown. Then fold each corner into the center.

3. Fold in half this way to crease.

4. Then unfold and fold in half the other way. Your cootie catcher is ready for labeling.

5. Stick both thumbs and pointer fingers into the four pockets. Push all the pockets to a point to begin playing.

Easy Answers

When test time comes, will you be headed in the right direction?

For this quiz, it's important to read all the directions before you begin answering questions. The questions might seem weird, but that's OK. If you do as directed, it'll be easy to earn a great score. Choose the best answer for the even-numbered questions. Make sure to select the silliest answer for each odd-numbered question.

1. Halloween is in October, and St. Patrick's Day is in March. When is the Fourth of July?

a. July
b. New Year's Eve
c. summertime

2. If you read two chapters of a book one day and three the next day, how many chapters did you read?

a. 4
b. 5
c. 6

3. Your teacher loves it when students . . .

a. turn in assignments on time.
b. come to class.
c. sing the alphabet song out loud in the middle of a spelling test.

4. At school, you're most likely to eat your lunch . . .

a. in the cafeteria.
b. in the teacher's lounge.
c. in the principal's office.

5. Paris is the capital of France. Mexico City is the capital of Mexico. The capital of the United States is . . .

a. Honolulu.
b. in the eastern part of the country.
c. Washington, D.C.

6. A good example of a healthy snack is . . .

a. marshmallows.
b. soda.
c. an apple.

7. How many letters are there in the word *directions*?

a. 10
b. Not as many as in the word *instructions*.
c. I can't count that high.

answers

Did you choose all **blue** answers? If not, you didn't follow the directions! If you read closely, you knew you were supposed to choose the correct answers for the even-numbered questions but the *silliest* answer for each odd-numbered question. Did you get fooled?

Carefully reading and following directions is the most important test-taking skill you'll ever learn! If you don't follow directions, you won't get the chance to show off all you know, no matter how hard you study.

TOP TIPS FOR TESTS

Follow these rules to bring your best to every test.

- **Be prepared.** Arrive to class a bit early on test day, and make sure you have any materials you need, including pencils, pens, and paper.

- **Read all directions** before you answer any questions.

- **Scan** through the whole test before you begin. Think about which parts of the test will be the most challenging and which parts will take the most time. Plan your test time accordingly.

- **Answer** questions you know first. Skip questions you don't know and come back to them later if you have time.

- **Use the test** as a resource! Sometimes you might find an answer you don't know hidden inside another question on the test.

- **Multiple choice?** Eliminate the choices you're sure are wrong and choose one of the remaining answers.

- **True or false?** Pay close attention to the words in the statement. Are they the same words your teacher used when talking about the topic? Keep in mind that just one false word can make a whole statement false.

- **Essay question?** Keywords in the question can tell you what is required in your answer, such as "give examples," "compare and contrast," or "list reasons why."

- **Don't rush!** You won't score extra points by being first to turn in your test.

- **Go for extra credit.** The worst that can happen is you don't score the points.

- **If you finish** with time to spare, make sure to check your answers. Read through your whole test—questions and answers—before you turn it in.

- **Relax!** Teachers don't expect you to do perfectly on every test. They just expect you to try to do your best.

ON THE FLIP SIDE

Nervous before a big test? Right before the exam begins, take a minute to write down what's on your mind. List your fears and worries. This simple exercise has been shown to improve test scores!

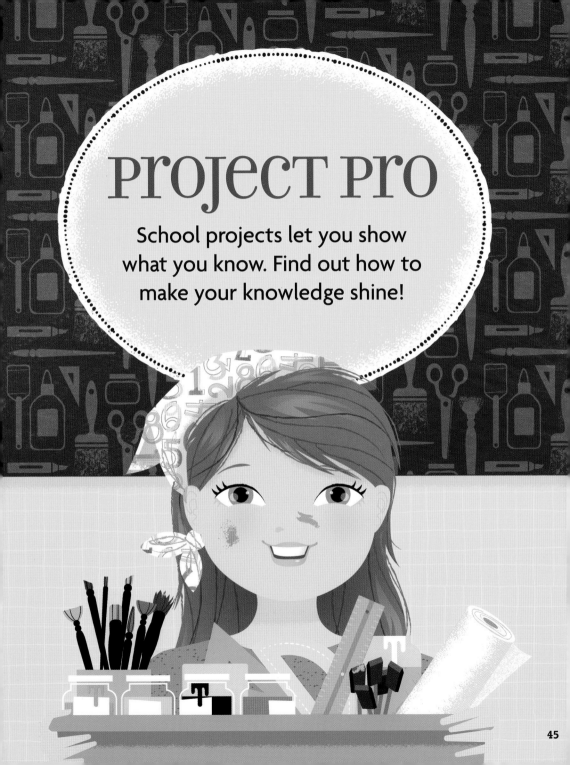

Project Pro

School projects let you show what you know. Find out how to make your knowledge shine!

TALENT SCOUT

When teachers assign school projects, sometimes it's hard to know where to begin. This quiz helps you discover what kinds of projects best suit *your* skills.

1. At school, you feel comfortable in . . .

    a. art class. Painting, drawing, sculpting—you love learning new ways to create.

    b. speech class. Pressure to perform brings out your best.

    c. writing lab. You have confidence working with words.

2. You'd wish your friend a happy birthday by . . .

    a. singing her a personalized birthday song.

    b. creating a card that shows things she loves.

    c. sending a letter telling her how much you appreciate her.

3. You're studying ancient Rome in history class. If the teacher put you in charge for the day, you'd instruct your classmates to . . .

    a. put together a report about a Roman emperor.

    b. put on skits about their favorite Roman gods and goddesses.

    c. build models of the Roman Colosseum.

4. The after-school activity you'd enjoy most is . . .

    a. craft club.

    b. the school play.

    c. the student newspaper.

5. If you kept a journal, it would be . . .

    a. typed on your computer.

    b. a video recording of your thoughts.

    c. a book you made by hand filled with doodles and dreams.

Answers

Did you select **orange** answers most? Choose projects that let you **write it!** You'll breeze through projects such as reports or stories where your words carry the weight.

Are your answers mostly **green?** Choose projects that let you **make it!** Your hands-on, creative side will steer you to success on posters, models, and food or craft projects.

Did you pick a lot of **purple** answers? Choose projects that let you **perform it!** Give a speech, put on a skit, dress up as a character from fiction or history, or host a quiz show to spotlight your project power.

Topic Testers

Trying to decide what your project should be about? Ask yourself these questions to narrow down your options:

- What do I know about?

- What do I want to learn more about?

- How does my topic relate to what we're learning in class?

- Is my topic too big? Too small? Just right?

- Will I be able to find information on this topic? How? Where?

Idea Factory

Brainstorm ideas for writing, projects, problem solving, and more.

When you need to choose a topic for a project or figure out the direction your project should take, brainstorming can help. In brainstorming, you think up and record ideas about a specific topic or in answer to a particular question. The goal of brainstorming is not to find the best idea or the most important idea. Instead, you're trying to come up with *as many ideas as you can,* and your ideas can cover a wide area around your topic or question.

Brainstorm Boundaries

- Set a timer, and don't stop coming up with ideas until it beeps!

- There are no bad ideas in brainstorming! Don't judge the ideas you come up with. Just write them down.

- Crazy ideas are OK, too! Something that seems strange in the moment might spur your best idea later on.

- Brainstorm alone or with a group.

Write Right

- Record your ideas in a list. Use categories to sort ideas.

- Create a mind map or a web. Write your brainstorm topic in the center of a blank page and circle it. Draw lines to connect new ideas to the topic and to each other.

- Freewrite—just keep writing until time is up, no matter what you put down on the page.

Idea Swap
Working in a group, brain-stormers list ideas on paper, then swap sheets after two minutes. Keep swapping until papers are full.

Flip It
Imagine you're arguing the opposite point to your own. How would you see things? What would you say?

Hunt for Headlines
If your topic were in the newspaper, what would the headline say? What would the story say?

Brainstorm Boosters

Imagine the Worst
List the worst outcomes or ideas you can think of. They'll help you see the best ideas.

Have Character
Imagine you're a character from a book, movie, or TV show. What would that character say about your topic?

Exaggerate!!!
Make it bigger, wilder, smaller, sillier. See what happens.

Back to Basics
What if no one had any idea what your brain-storm topic was or what it meant? How would you explain it?

Group Dynamics

When your teacher assigns a group project,
what part do you play in getting the job done?

1. Your class is planning a field trip to a nature center. You'd choose to . . .

   a. help make sandwiches for the group's picnic lunch.

   b. lead the group on a hike.

   c. plan a nature scavenger hunt.

2. In the science lab, you're most likely to be the student who . . .

   a. designs your group's experiment.

   b. gathers supplies for your group's experiment.

   c. carefully records the results of your group's experiment.

3. Your teacher asks students to plan the class Valentine's party. You'd volunteer to . . .

   a. organize sign-up for snacks and supplies.

   b. teach your classmates how to fold origami Valentines.

   c. cut out paper hearts to prep for a game.

4. You love basketball, so you join your school's team. Your teammates nominate you to . . .

   a. organize the practice schedule.

   b. help sweep the gym before practice.

   c. call the plays at practice.

5. On your report card, your teacher might praise the way you . . .

   a. follow directions and do a thorough job on homework.

   b. keep a detailed assignment calendar.

   c. set a good example for other students by speaking up for what's right.

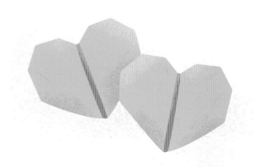

Answers

If you picked **red** the most, you're a worker bee. You never mind pitching in on any job—large or small—that the group needs. Your classmates can count on you to give your best effort until a project is complete. Keep in mind that your ideas and opinions can help your group just as much as your hard work.

If your answers are mostly **purple**, you're a planner and organizer. You'll help your project group stick to a schedule. You'll make sure each person has a job to do. Try not to be too rigid in your plans. Some group members will prefer working with more flexibility than you do.

If you chose a lot of **blue** answers, you're a natural group leader. You don't mind taking charge and leading a team in the right direction, and you're not afraid to make decisions. Just make sure that you are open to ideas from everyone in your group—be responsible, not rude.

Be a Team Player

No matter what role you fill, keep these tips in mind whenever you work with other students:

- **Listen.** When others are speaking, really listen to what they say. Don't interrupt or dismiss others' ideas.

- **Compromise** and be flexible. If you want all group members to contribute work, you need to let them all contribute plans and ideas.

- Give each group member a chance to use her **best talents.** If one person is a fantastic artist, let her make your poster; if another loves the library, put her in charge of research.

- Don't let your group down. If you say you'll do something, **get it done.** Others are counting on you!

Just The Facts

Tech tools make it easier than ever to do research and find information. But how can you tell if the information you find is factual? Follow this flowchart to figure it out.

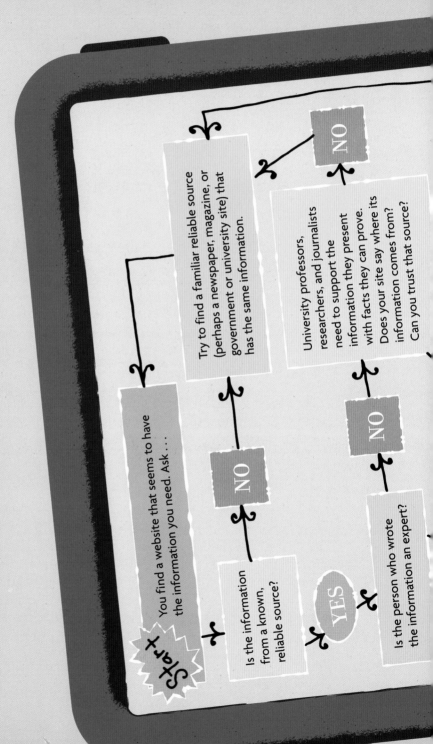

Start

You find a website that seems to have the information you need. Ask . . .

Is the information from a known, reliable source?

NO

Try to find a familiar reliable source (perhaps a newspaper, magazine, or government or university site) that has the same information.

NO

YES

Is the person who wrote the information an expert?

NO

University professors, researchers, and journalists need to support the information they present with facts they can prove. Does your site say where its information comes from? Can you trust that source?

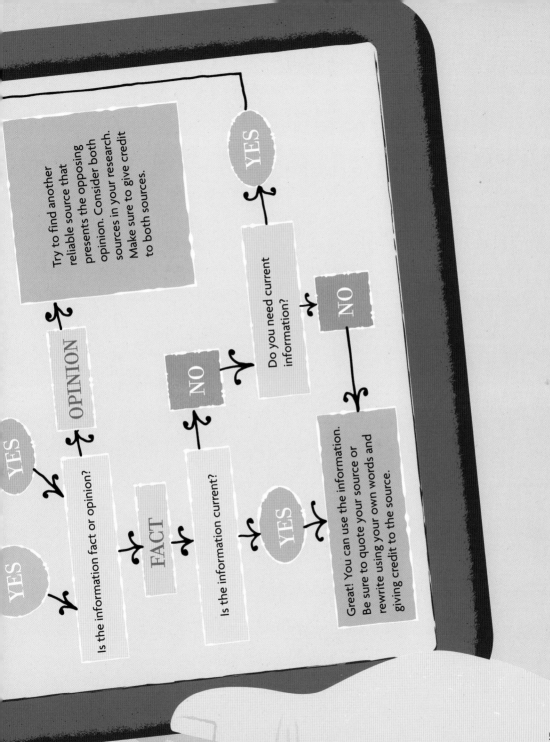

Try to find another reliable source that presents the opposing opinion. Consider both sources in your research. Make sure to give credit to both sources.

YES

Do you need current information?

NO

OPINION

NO

Is the information fact or opinion?

YES

YES

FACT

Is the information current?

YES

Great! You can use the information. Be sure to quote your source or rewrite using your own words and giving credit to the source.

YES

Research RIGHT

If you are still not sure if you've found a good source, ask your teacher. Better yet, **ask a librarian!** Librarians love to help students find information and are experts with different types of media sources—including the Internet.

GOOD NIGHT, SLEEP TIGHT

Test your sleep smarts with this quick quiz.

1. How much sleep do kids ages 8–12 need every night to do their best at school?

   a. About 10 to 11 hours
   b. About 8 to 9 hours
   c. At least 7 hours

2. When you're busy with homework and activities and you don't get as much sleep as you should during the week, it's fine to make up for lost ZZZs by sleeping late on the weekends.

   True   **False**

3. Your piano recital is tomorrow, and you want to perfect your song, but you're pretty tired and it's already late. To play your best for the show you should . . .

   a. just go to bed and try to relax.
   b. stay up for a short practice session but sleep until your regular time in the morning.
   c. get up early to practice before the recital starts.

4. You have a vocabulary test tomorrow, and you need to review your words. But you're tired and it's your bedtime. To do your best on your test you should . . .

   a. force yourself to stay up a bit later to cram the definitions.
   b. get up half an hour early to review your words in the morning.
   c. skip the studying and just go to bed.

5. Naps cannot help you focus for studying and homework. By the time you're in grade school, you're too old for naps!

   True   **False**

dream BIG

You need sleep to feel sharp in school. But that's not the only way sleep helps you learn. Brain scientists say that sleep helps you see the big picture and make connections between all the new information you take in each day. What a great reason not to skimp on sleep!

Answers

1. a

Believe it or not, doctors recommend that grade-school-aged kids need 10 to 11 hours of sleep every night to stay healthy and alert. So if you have to wake up at 7, you should try to go to sleep between 8 and 9.

2. False

If you sleep late on the weekends, you make it hard for your body to wake up alert and refreshed on Monday morning. Try not to sleep more than one hour past your weekday wake-up time on the weekends.

3. b

Sleep scientists say the kind of sleep your body gets at the end of your sleep cycle really helps you when you need to perform. So, if you're playing in a big game or putting on a show, try to get up at your normal time.

4. b

If you're tired, staying up to study is not the best use of your time. Your sleepy, sluggish brain won't remember the information you're reviewing as well as it could. So go to bed, but wake up half an hour early to study. When your brain is refreshed by sleep, the information you study is more likely to stick.

5. False

A quick nap can help improve your study focus—you'll do better work with a little rest. However, try not to nap for longer than 20 or 30 minutes. If you nap too long, you might feel super groggy when you get back to work. And don't nap after around 4 p.m. If you nap late in the day, you might have a hard time falling asleep at bedtime.

Brain Bites

Sink your teeth into these superfoods that actually make your brain work better!

Eggs are great for your memory!

Avocados provide healthy fats that help you concentrate. Bring on the guacamole!

Oatmeal gives your brain energy that lasts all morning.

Bananas can boost your mood and give your brain fuel to learn.

Berries are packed with vitamins that can help your brain run smoothly.

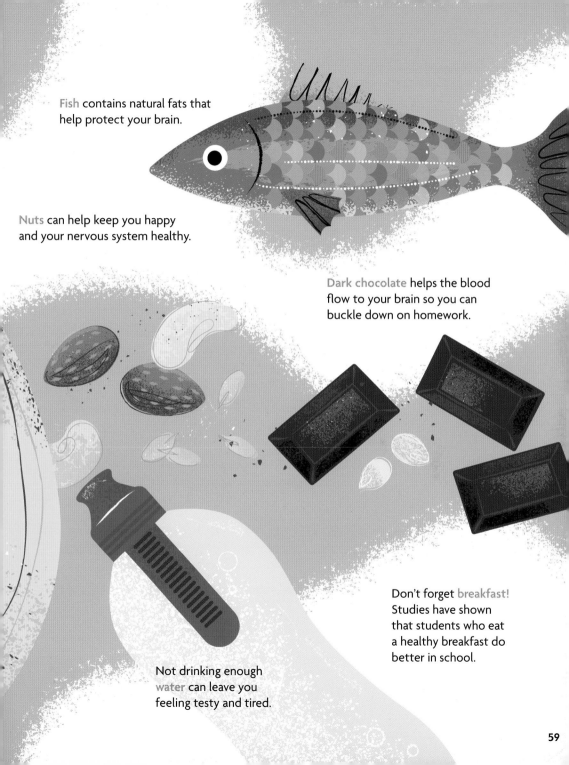

Fish contains natural fats that help protect your brain.

Nuts can help keep you happy and your nervous system healthy.

Dark chocolate helps the blood flow to your brain so you can buckle down on homework.

Don't forget breakfast! Studies have shown that students who eat a healthy breakfast do better in school.

Not drinking enough water can leave you feeling testy and tired.

POWER LUNCH

Need some healthy inspiration to shake up your school lunch?
Choose at least one food from each column to pack the perfect sack!

VEGGIES	FRUITS	PROTEINS	GRAINS	TREATS
carrots and dip	apple	peanut butter	whole-grain bread	dried fruit
broccoli	grapes	eggs (hard-boiled or cooked like an omelet and cooled)	whole-grain tortilla	yogurt-covered raisins
spinach and dressing	strawberries	lunch meat	whole-grain crackers	yogurt drink
cherry tomatoes	banana	edamame	whole-grain dry cereal	dark chocolate
cucumber slices	blueberries	nuts	oatmeal	homemade granola
celery	orange	cold chicken	whole-grain pita chips	chocolate milk
snap peas	peach	cheese	air-popped popcorn	
cauliflower	pear	hummus	bran muffin	
pepper slices	pineapple chunks	beans		

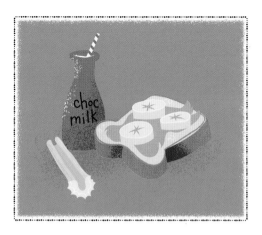

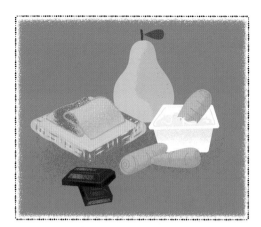

TRY OUT THESE
Brain-BOOSTING
COMBOS

NUTTY PROFESSOR
peanut butter + banana + chocolate
chips + whole-wheat tortilla

SMARTY SALAD
spinach + raspberries + almonds
+ chicken chunks

MIND MUNCH TRAIL MIX
whole-grain cereal + nuts
+ dried blueberries

CLEVER CUKE
hummus + cucumber slices +
turkey lunch meat
+ whole-wheat tortilla

PROBLEM SOLVING

Find solutions to problems that crop up in class and at home.

fair and square?

You know it's wrong to cheat at school. But it can be confusing to figure out what counts as cheating. Circle answers to see if you can tell what crosses the line from fair game to foul play.

1. You find a perfect explanation of your science fair project online, so you copy the text right onto your poster.

Fair Game   Foul Play

2. You and your study buddy work together to find definitions for your vocabulary words.

Fair Game   Foul Play

3. You're writing a report on France, and you use your computer to create maps and an image of the French flag.

Fair Game   Foul Play

4. You're having a hard time on your math test, and you're worried you won't get done before class ends. You glance up at the clock, and you realize you can see right onto another student's paper. She's a math whiz! You check to see if your answers are the same as hers.

Fair Game   Foul Play

5. Last night you had soccer practice, a piano lesson, and your brother's birthday dinner. You just didn't have time to finish your grammar homework. You ask your friend if you can copy her paper, just this one time. It's only homework—not a test or anything.

Fair Game   **Foul Play**

6. You don't understand how to do your math homework, so you ask your mom for help. She ends up solving half the problems for you.

Fair Game   **Foul Play**

7. You didn't finish reading the novel your teacher assigned over spring break. So, the night before you go back to school, you search the Internet for a summary of the book. You write your book report based on what you read online.

Fair Game   **Foul Play**

Answers

1. **Foul Play.** Presenting someone else's words or ideas as your own is called *plagiarism* (PLAY-juh-rihs-um), and it's *definitely* cheating. When you use someone else's exact words, use quotation marks and tell who said the words. When you put someone else's idea into your own words, give credit to the source of the idea.

2. **It depends.** Sometimes teachers assign students to work together. If that's the case, then working or studying with a partner and sharing information and answers is A-OK. But most of the time, teachers expect each student to do her own work. If you know that your teacher assumes you will complete an assignment on your own, then it is cheating to share answers with a friend.

3. **Fair Game.** Tech tools like computers help make homework a breeze. It's not cheating to use a computer as a tool to make your work better. It is cheating to use a computer to copy words, diagrams, maps, or other information directly from the Internet and present them as your own work.

4. **Foul Play.** It's always cheating to peek at another student's paper, even if you can hardly help seeing it. Keep your eyes on your own work.

5. **Foul Play.** Copying homework is cheating, even if you only do it *just one time*. Teachers understand that once in a while, family obligations may prevent you from finishing your homework. When it happens to you, talk to your teacher to figure out a plan to make up the work.

6. Foul Play. Parents can be a great resource when you get stuck on schoolwork. And sometimes parents get really excited to help out. But it's your job not to let your parents complete your work for you. How can you learn if you don't do the work yourself?

7. Foul Play. Information on the Internet can be a useful homework helper. But using a shortcut like reading a summary of a book instead of the book itself is cheating. Think of it this way: You're acting as if you read the book when really you did not. That's lying.

ABOUT CHEATING

Have you ever done anything that could be considered cheating? How did it make you feel? What would you do differently?

It's good to have a plan in case you ever feel tempted to cheat. If that happened to you, what would you do to avoid it?

A WAY WITH WORDS

In order to get help solving problems, you've got to speak up for yourself! Challenge yourself to choose the right words, and you'll talk your way through your troubles.

WHEN YOU'RE TALKING TO A TEACHER . . .

INSTEAD OF SAYING
"I just don't get it!"

TRY
"I don't understand how this problem works. Could you please explain it to me again?"

or

"I'm having a hard time finding the answers to these questions. I read the chapter, but I still need help. Could you point me in the right direction?"

INSTEAD OF SAYING
"I can't believe you gave my essay a C. Your grades are never fair!"

TRY
"I'd really appreciate it if you could explain why you gave my essay a C. I'd like to understand what I need to do better next time."

INSTEAD OF SAYING

"Of course I don't have my homework. You never even told us that was part of the assignment."

TRY

"I'm sorry. I must have mis-understood the assignment. Could you please give me an extra day to complete it?"

WHEN YOU'RE TALKING TO A PARENT . . .

INSTEAD OF SAYING
"Mr. Whistler is such a jerk! He picks on me in class, and he's never fair. He's the worst."

TRY
"I'm having a hard time getting along with Mr. Whistler. I feel like he picks on me and doesn't treat me fairly. Could you give me some advice?"

INSTEAD OF SAYING
"Back off! I'm not a baby anymore!"

TRY
"I want to take more responsibility for my school-work. I feel like you check in on everything I do. I've shown I'm responsible by earning good grades and following the rules. Can I have some space?"

INSTEAD OF SAYING
"Too much homework! I quit!"

TRY
"I'm having a hard time handling my homework and activities and all my other responsibilities right now. Could you help me figure out what to do?"

ASKING FOR HELP

You're going on a family vacation, and you'll be absent for several days. You need to ask your teacher for the homework you'll miss. What could you say?

You're proud to be a good student. Lately, though, some friends have started teasing you for doing well at school. They're calling you "nerd" and "teacher's pet." You want to talk to your parents about what's going on. What could you say?

Whatever problem you face, be clear and courteous when you ask for help. Calmly give details about how you're feeling and how you see the situation. Take responsibility for your role in solving problems—don't expect others to do the work for you. And know that everyone needs help from time to time!

STRESS TEST

Does the pressure to be perfect leave you feeling overwhelmed?
Circle your answers to see what worries you.

1. Sometimes tests make me feel so nervous, I know I don't perform my best.

Sounds like me.   That's not me.

2. With all my homework, projects, sports, and clubs, I never get a chance to relax or do what I want to do. It's really stressing me out!

Sounds like me.   That's not me.

3. Sometimes I can't sleep at night. I just lie in bed awake, worrying about school.

Sounds like me.   That's not me.

4. I have to do well on every assignment, quiz, and test or my teachers and parents will probably think I'm not smart.

Sounds like me.   That's not me.

5. My friends want me to help them cheat. I know it's wrong, but I don't want them to be mad at me.

Sounds like me.   That's not me.

answers

Did you answer "Sounds like me" for any of the questions? If so, you feel stressed about school, at least once in a while. The next time pressure builds, try one of the tips below to find peace and perspective.

- **Take a deep breath.** Hold it for a few seconds. Let it out as slowly as you can. Repeat several times, concentrating on how it feels to breathe in and out.

- **Ask yourself some questions:** How important is the thing I'm worried about? Will I care what happens in a week? Will I care in a year? What's the worst that will happen if things don't turn out as I want them to?

- **Take a break from your schoolwork.** Go for a walk, play a game, eat a healthy snack, do some yoga, or take a 20-minute nap. Reevaluate how you feel about your work before you begin again.

- **Write down the problem that's bothering you.** Make a list of ways you might solve the problem. If you're feeling stressed about *how much* schoolwork you have to do, make a master list of all the tasks you need to complete. Check off each job as you get it done.

- **Talk to someone you trust about your feelings!** Chat with a friend, a sibling, a teacher, or your mom or dad and ask for advice on how to handle your stressful situation.

EXTra CreDIT

Put together your own team for school support. Copy this chart into your assignment notebook or planner and then fill it in.

TODAY _____

SUBJECT	WHEN I NEED	I'LL ASK

THINGS TO REMEMBER

a super-smart study buddy
KYLE

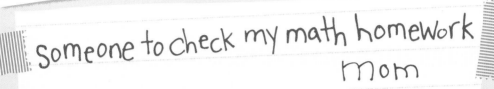

Someone to check my math homework
mom

help finding information for
a research Project   MRS.
                      Welch

a partner to review flash cards
with me   Keegan

Someone to help me organize my
schoolwork   Taylor

a really good laugh
              Socks

help handling school stress
Dad

SCHOOL SPIRIT

Choose your school skills to earn an A for effort!

1. My favorite way to prepare for tests is to . . .

a. plan out what I need to review every night for the week before my test, and stick to my plan.

b. find a friend to quiz me on the material.

c. create a fun trivia game with all the information I've learned for the test.

2. I'm proud of my schoolwork because . . .

a. it's always organized, neat, and well prepared.

b. if I don't know the answers or how to do an assignment, I'm great at using the Internet, books, and other resources to figure it out.

c. I'm good at finding creative ways to show what I've learned.

3. Of all the kids in my class, my friends would say I'm the one most likely to . . .

a. never forget my homework or miss an assignment deadline.

b. bring in books from the library to support our studies or invite a speaker to share with the class.

c. find answers to problems and questions that even the teacher didn't think of.

4. If I don't do as well as I expected on an assignment or test, I try to improve the next time by . . .

a. correcting my work and planning extra study time for the areas where I made mistakes.

b. asking for help figuring out the topics that feel tricky to me.

c. brainstorming a new approach to the problems that challenged me and tackling those problems again with my fresh perspective.

5. I enjoy putting effort into . . .

a. keeping organized and on top of all my school subjects and activities.

b. working with classmates and my teacher to really understand the subjects I'm studying.

c. thinking about how everything I'm learning at school relates and using those connections to come up with new ideas of my own.

Answers

Did you choose any a's?

You've got a talent for organization! You know that putting effort into planning your schoolwork gives you the time and space you need to do your best.

Did you choose any b's?

You're resourceful! You're never afraid to ask for help. You know that having the right information—and help—when you need it lets your effort shine.

Did you choose any c's?

You're a creative thinker! You love putting effort into seeing things in a new way or presenting what you've learned with flair.

No matter which answers seemed most like you, here's something true: **The more you put into school, the more you will get out of it.** Your strong effort and positive attitude can take school from good to great. Let your school spirit shine!

TELL US HOW *YOU* RULE AT SCHOOL!

Super Secret Stuff!

STUDY secrets

TESTING TIPS

Lunches & Snack ideas

organizing tricks

& any OTHER ADVICE

write to us!

School Rules! Editor
American Girl
8400 Fairway Place
Middleton WI 53562

(Sorry, but photos can't be returned.
All comments and suggestions received
by American Girl may be used without
compensation or acknowledgment.)

Here are some other American Girl® books you might like:

Each sold separately. Find more books online at americangirl.com.

Discover online games, quizzes, activities,
and more at **americangirl.com/play**